I0791285

This Book Belongs to

____

Dedicated to

My Husband and Four precious gems Aakash, Adithya, Abishek and Sparsha. You make me so proud. Always be the best you can be.
-Mommy

Credits
Pictures from Google.com labeled for reuse, Bing.com All creative commons, Pixabay. Info from Wildlife fact files

STINGRAY

Content   Page

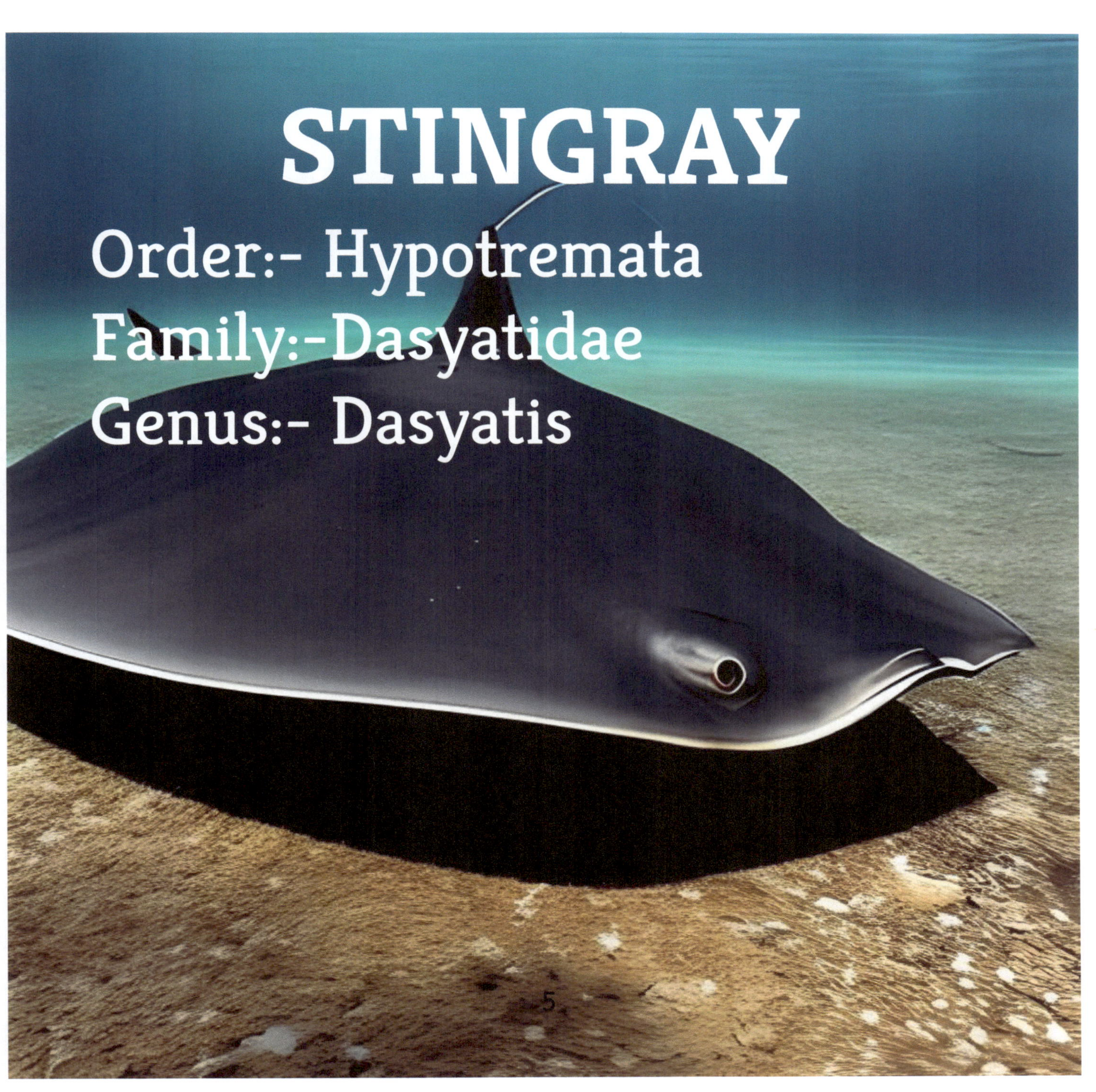
STINGRAY
Order:- Hypotremata
Family:-Dasyatidae
Genus:- Dasyatis
5

STINGRAY

Size:-
Width- Depends on the species
From 1-15 Ft
Length about 14 Ft
Weight:- 1-750 lb

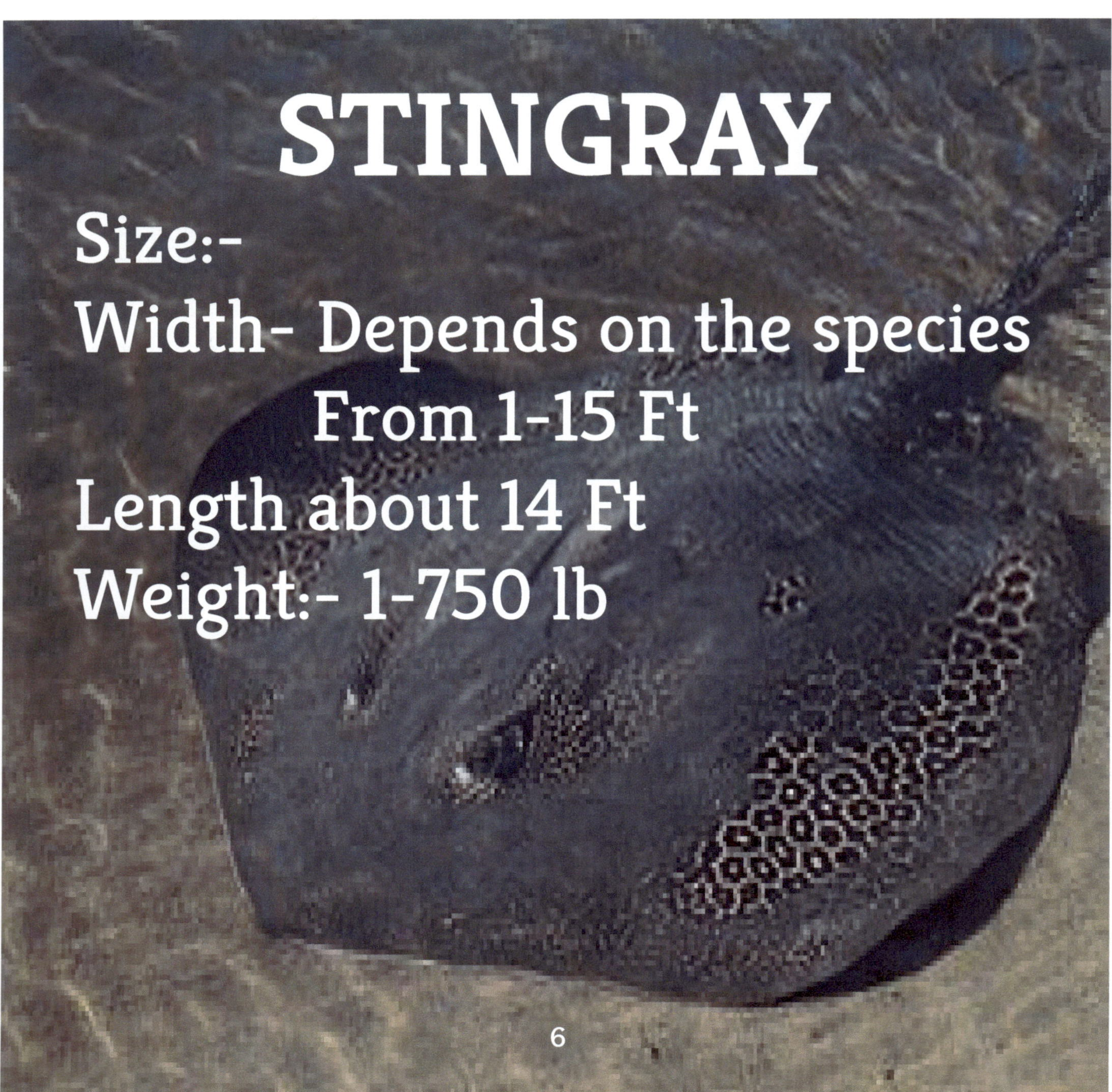

STINGRAY

They are usually rectangular to circular in shape and have spots on them

STINGRAY
Some have mottled marking
seen on them
8

STINGRAY
The name stingray is because of the sting they give their predators
9

STINGRAY

The stingray sting is located on its long whiplike spin that looks like tail that is in the rear end of the fish

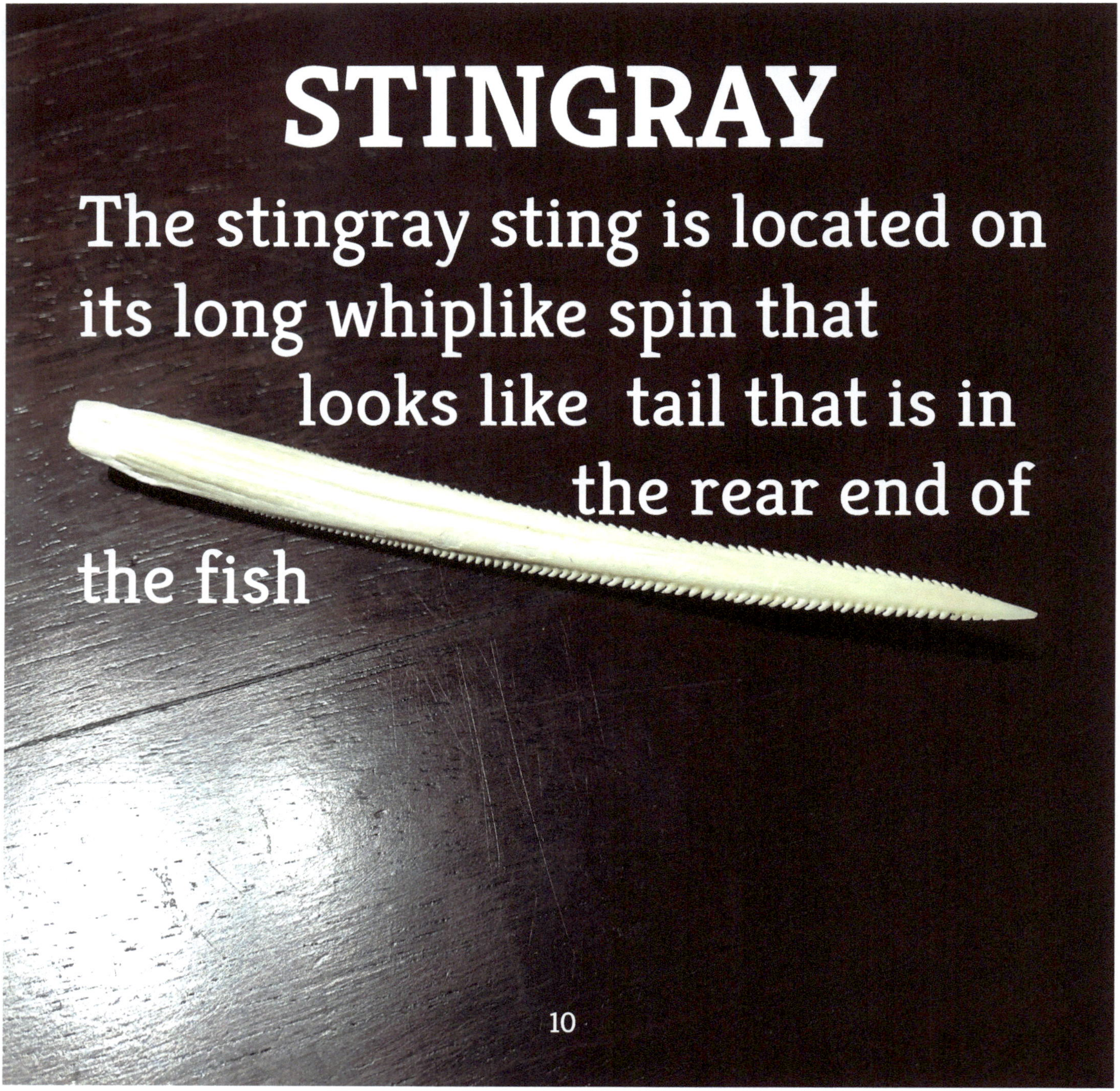

STINGRAY

When the stingray feels its being disturb or attacked it just lashes out its tail along with its spine from side to side as a defense mechanism

STINGRAY
The tail is flexible and acts like a defensive weapon to save itself from predators and to get its prey
12

STINGRAY

Its sting can kill an unsuspecting swimmer that is unaware of it or who is simply swimming and passing by

STINGRAY

<u>Habit:</u>

They love to live in shallow water

And love to be buried in soft sand in the beds of the sea or the river

STINGRAY

<u>Habit:</u>
They are active swimmers and move rapidly with a wing like fins that stretch on both sides

STINGRAY

Food and Feeding:

Stingrays feed on worms which are located at the bottom of the sea

STINGRAY

Food and Feeding:
They feed on mollusks and
that's one of its favorite food

STINGRAY
Food and Feeding:
They feed on crustaceans that
are availabe around it

STINGRAY

Food and Feeding:
Larger stingrays feed on dead
fish and squids that are
floating or have sunk in the sea

STINGRAY

<u>Food and Feeding:</u>
Stingrays mouth is on the underside of its body which is unlike other fish

STINGRAY

<u>Food and Feeding:</u>
Its wide jaw and several rows of blunt broad teeth is used to crush the shells which will be easy for digestion

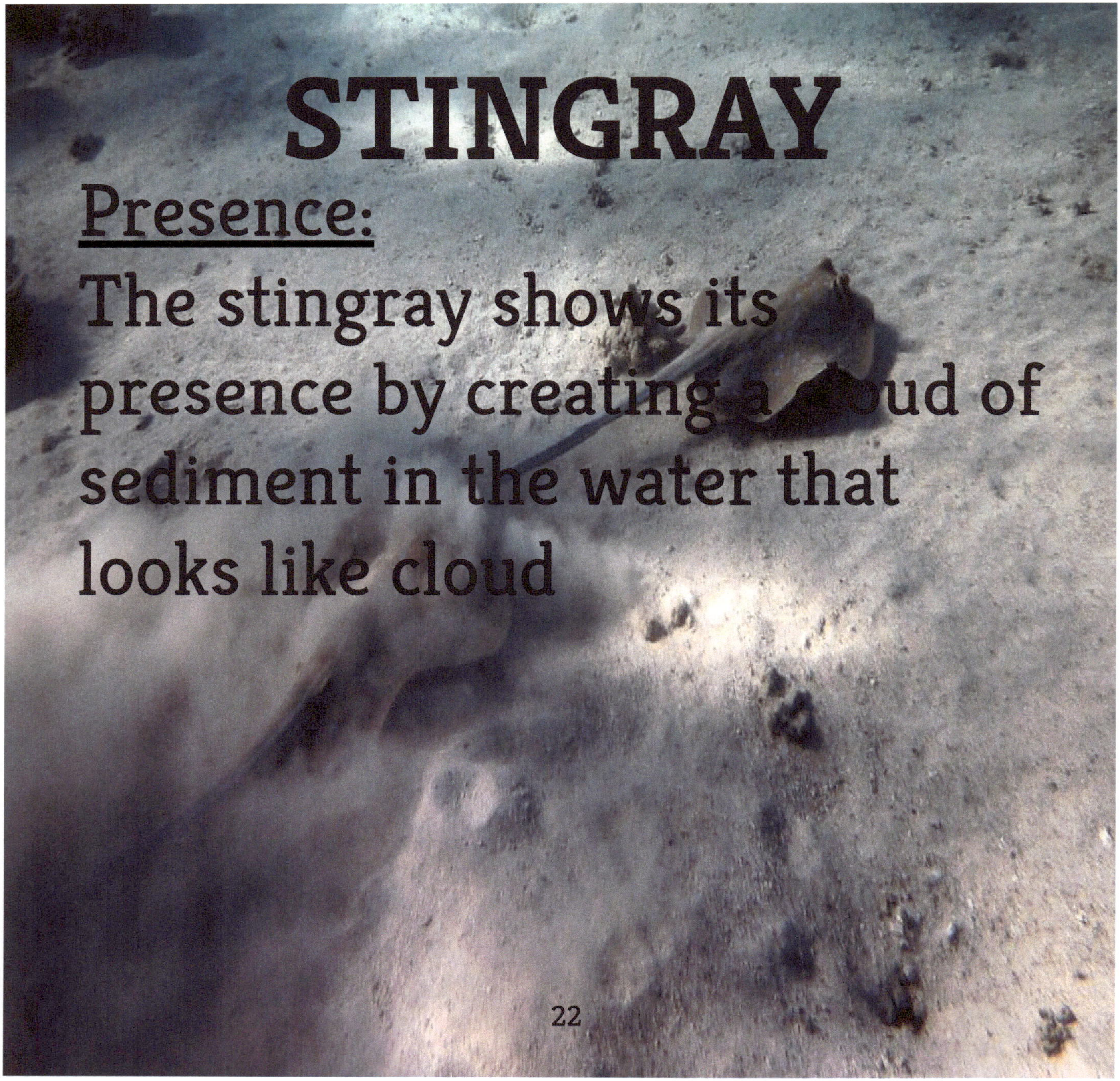

STINGRAY

<u>Presence:</u>

The stingray shows its presence by creating a cloud of sediment in the water that looks like cloud

STINGRAY

Species:
Common stingrays in North
and South America is the
Americana

23

STINGRAY

Species:

Common stingrays in Indian Ocean is the huge brevicaudata which is 14 feet in length

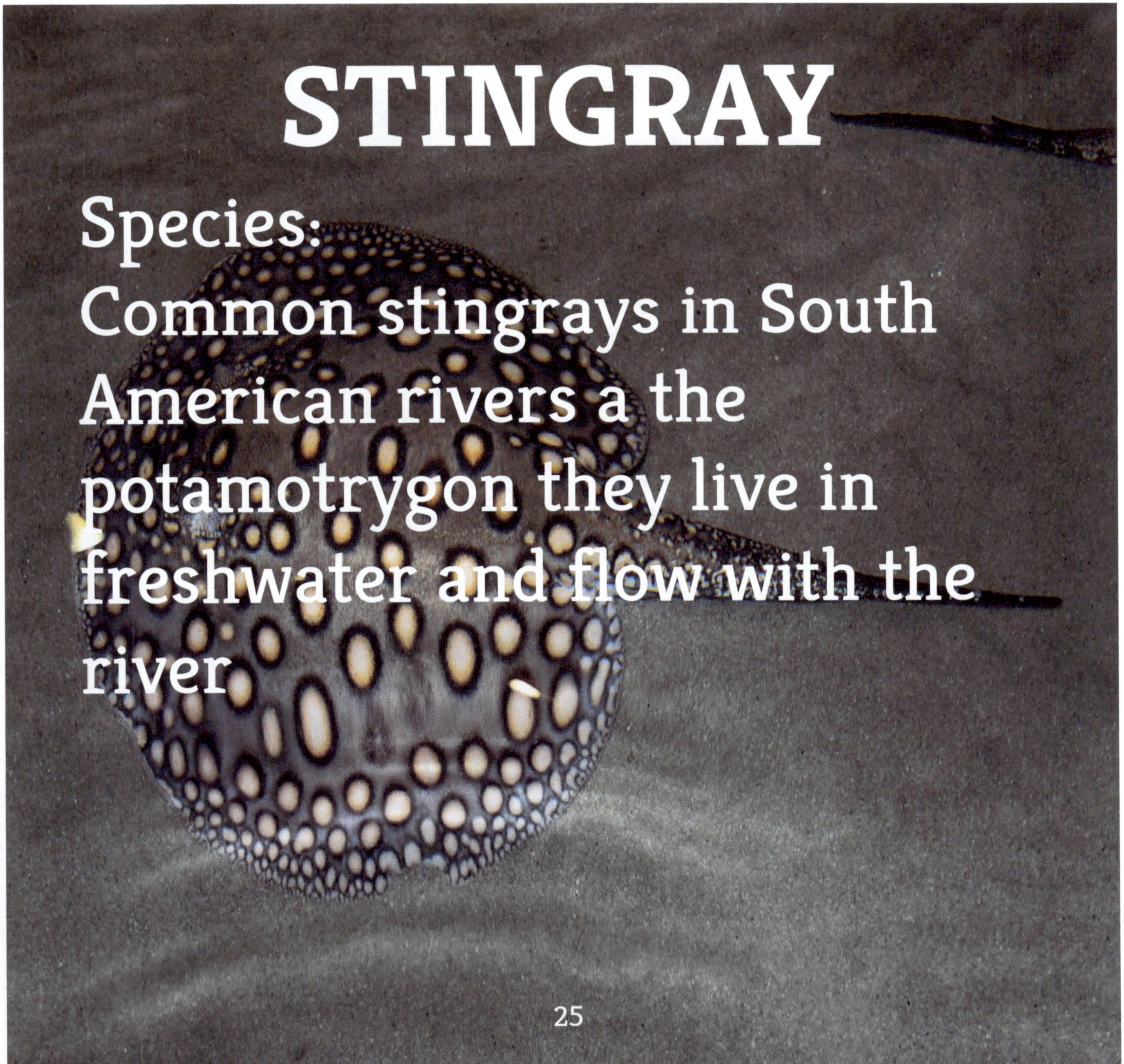

STINGRAY

Species:
Common stingrays in South American rivers a the potamotrygon they live in freshwater and flow with the river

STINGRAY

Breeding:
They produce 2 to 9 young ones which hatch from the female stingray's body like the other fish

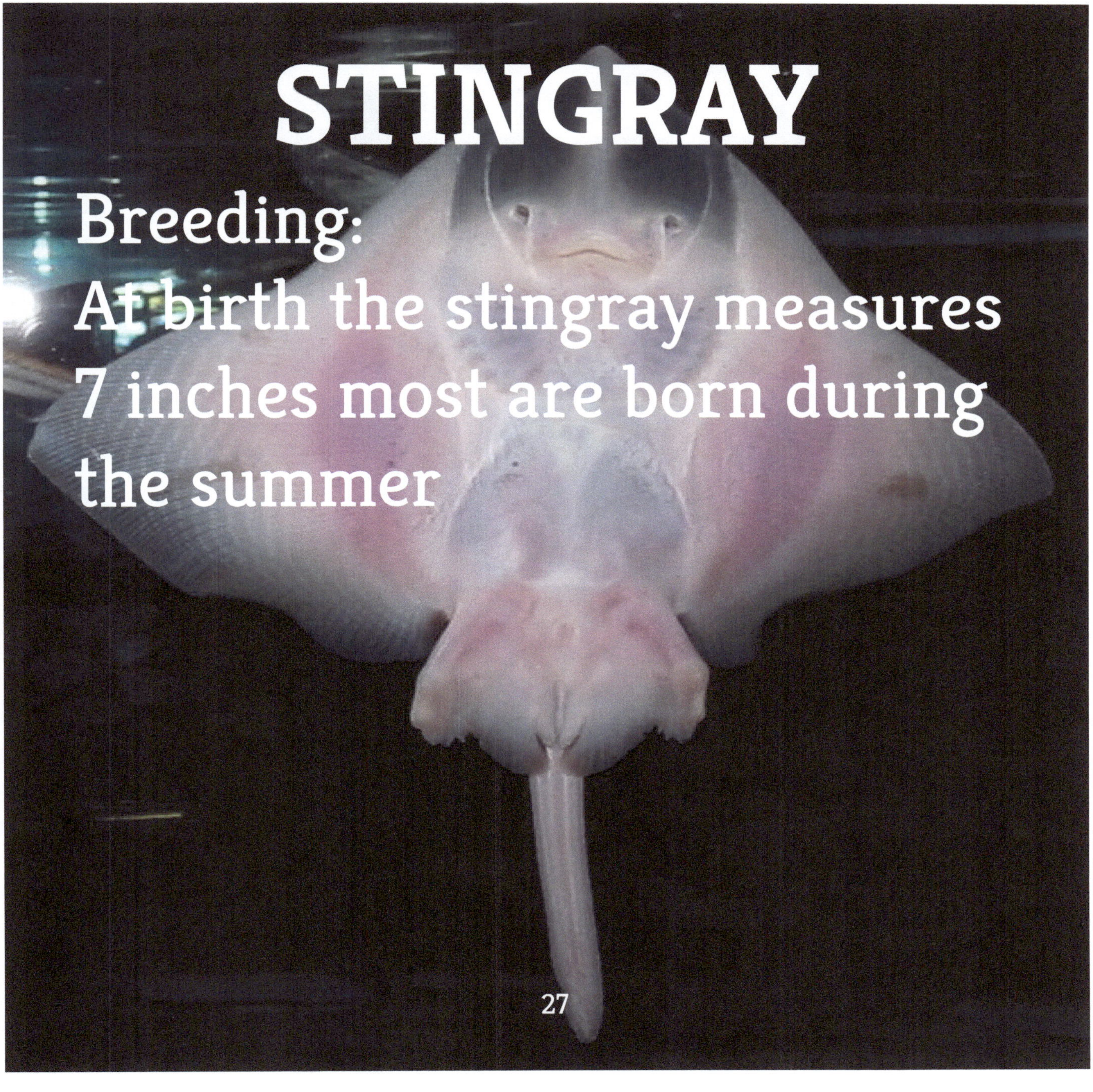

STINGRAY

Breeding:
At birth the stingray measures 7 inches most are born during the summer

STINGRAY

Benefits for man:
People hunt the stingray for its meat to eat,spine as a defensive weapon and its oil for medical purpose

STINGRAY

Disadvantages for man:
People are killed by some stingrays that are buried in the sand and which are unnoticed

STINGRAY
Disadvantages for man:
Stingrays raid the oyster and
shell farms for oyster
30

STINGRAY

Interesting Fact:

When stingrays are caught in the fishing nets the fishermen usually cut of the spine of the stingray and throw them back into the water

STINGRAY

<u>Interesting Fact:</u>

Hammerhead shark often prey on the stingrays.
The eyes in the hammerhead is used to see in clear water to trap the stingray and escape from the lashes of the stingray's whiplash

STINGRAY

Interesting Fact:
In Mexican waters hundreds of stingrays gather together into the seabed depressions known as ray pits

STINGRAY

<u>Interesting Fact:</u>
The oil extracted from stingray is used to prevent pneumonia or any kind of lung infection

STINGRAY

Notes

STINGRAY

Notes

Thank you for reading
about this swift swimmer
the stingray.
Hope you enjoyed it.
Check out our next book
All about Mandrill